How Many Toys?

by Anne Diorio

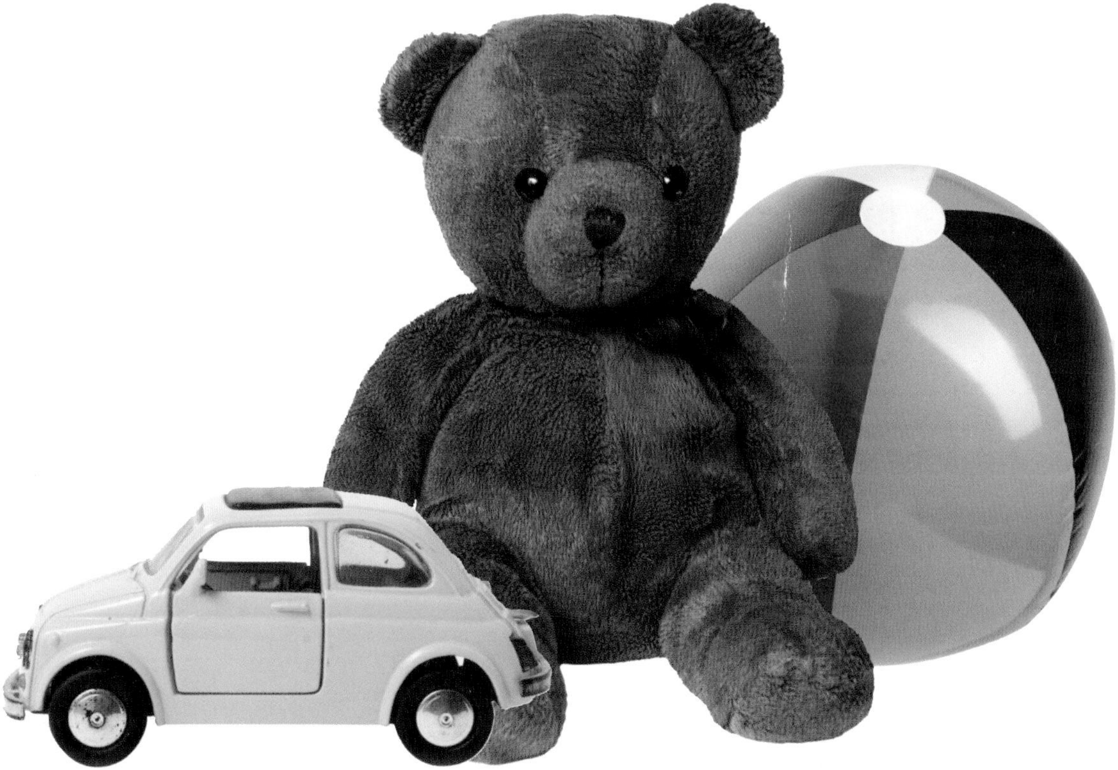

I have 1 doll.

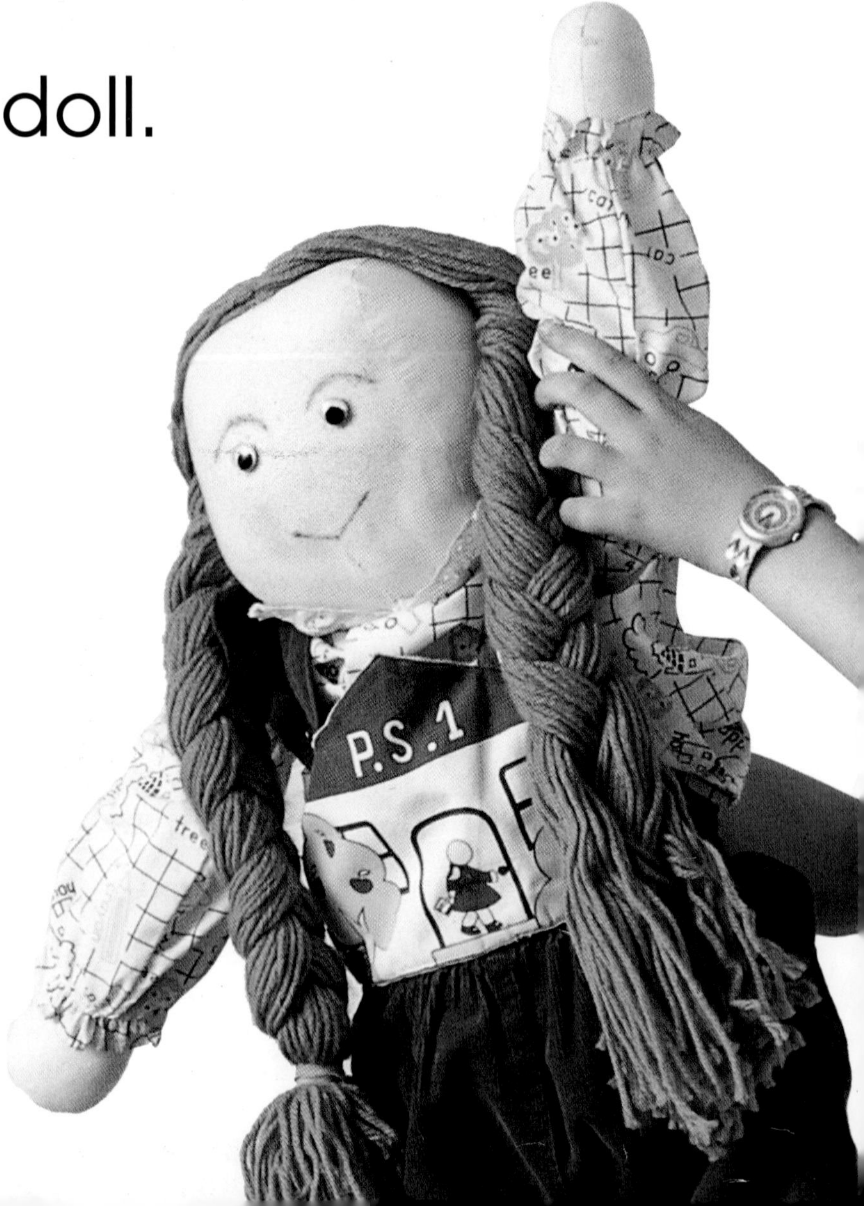

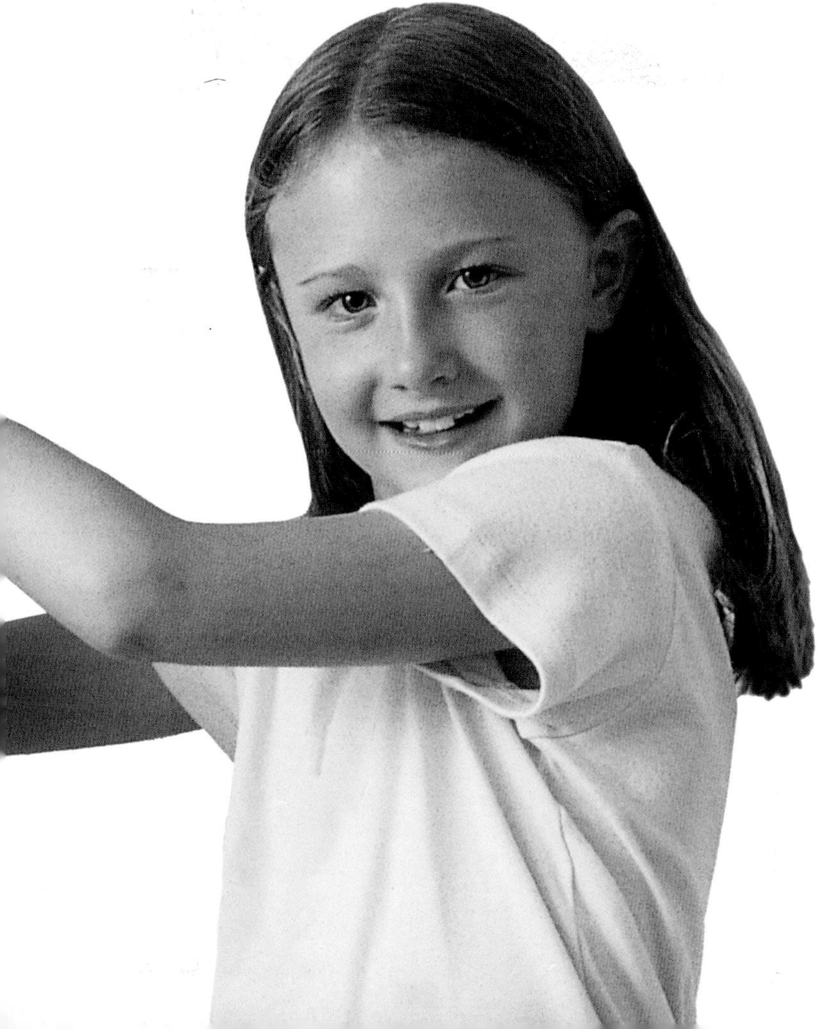

I have 2 bears.

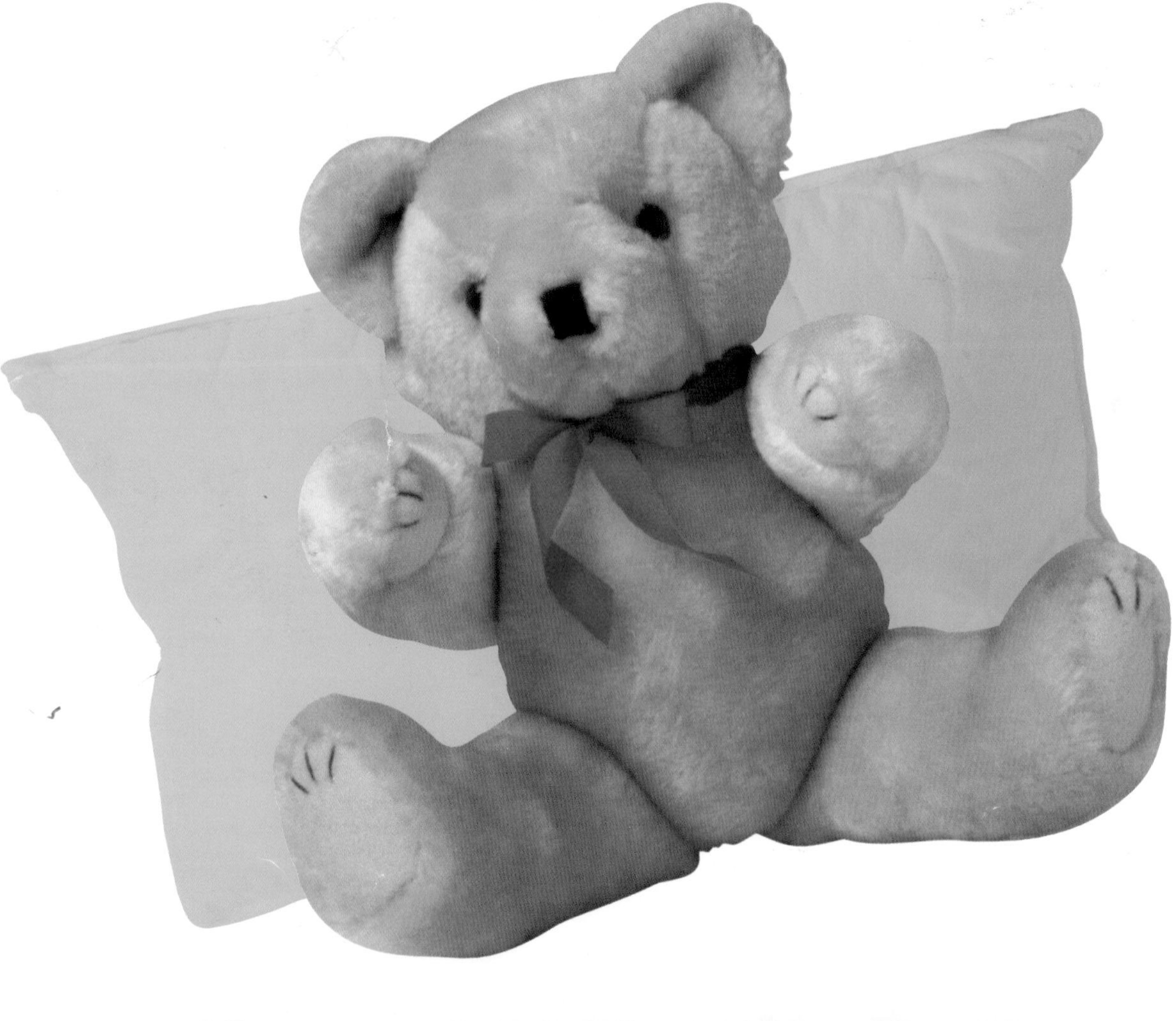

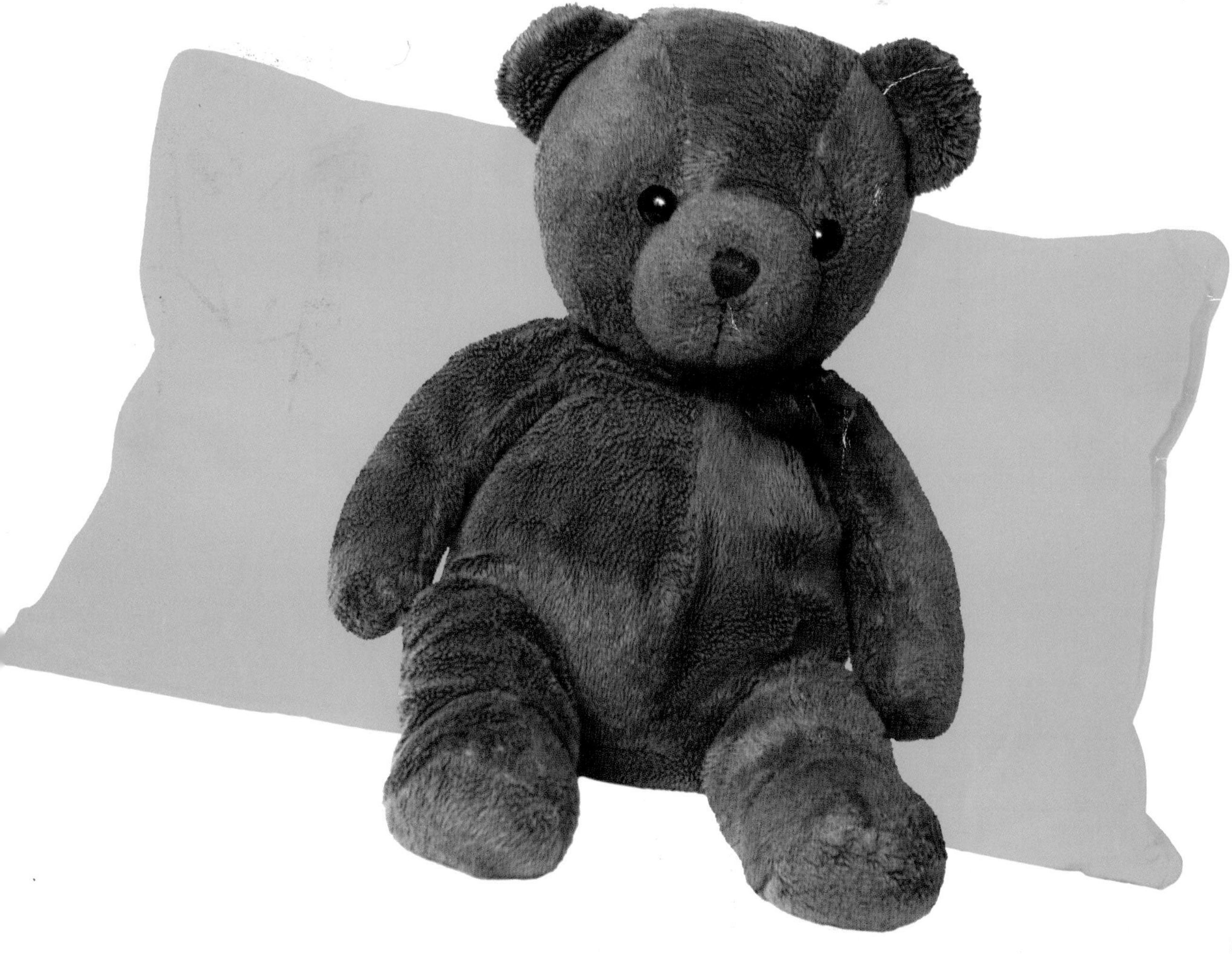

I have 3 balls.

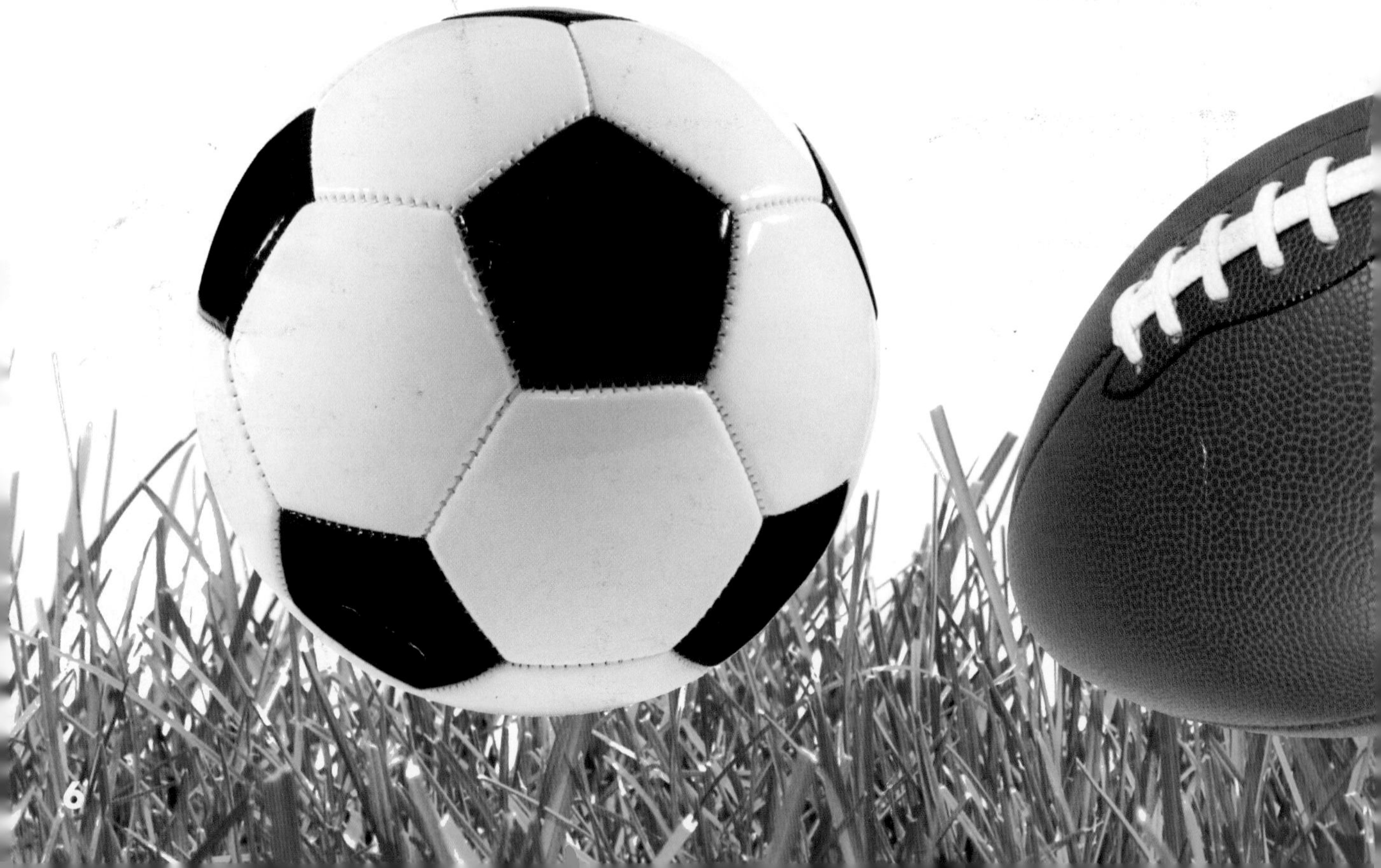

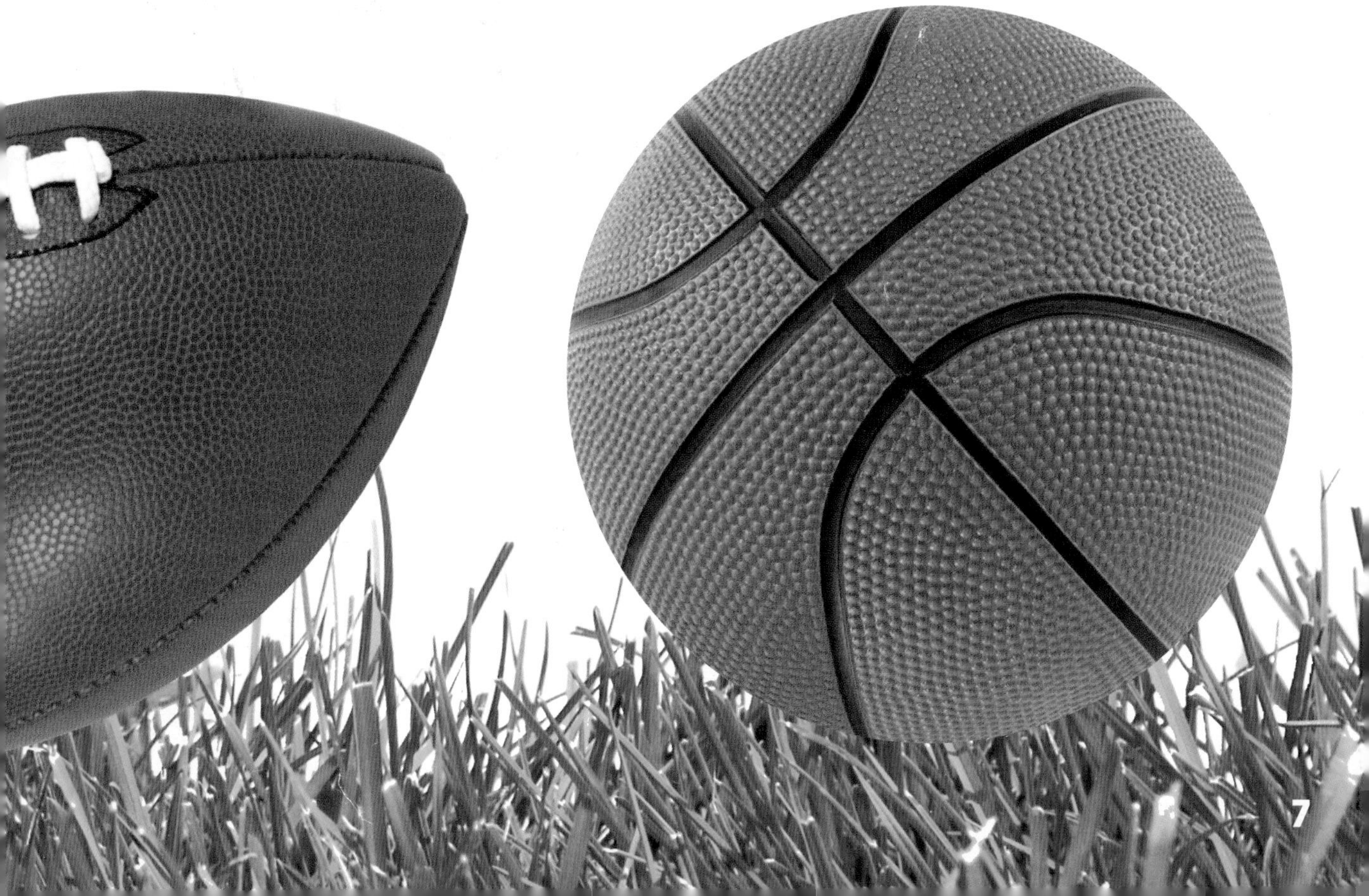

I have 4 cars.

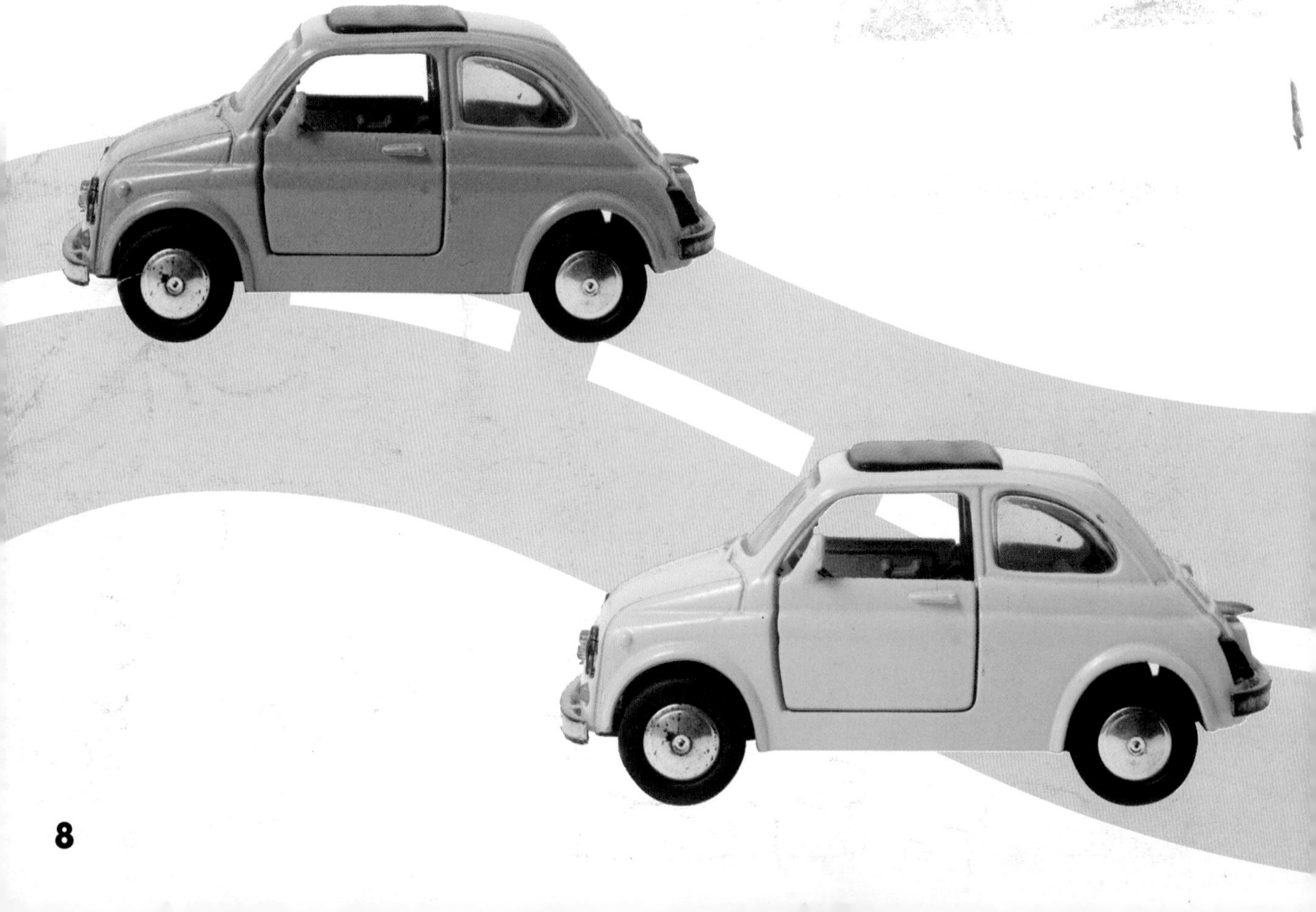

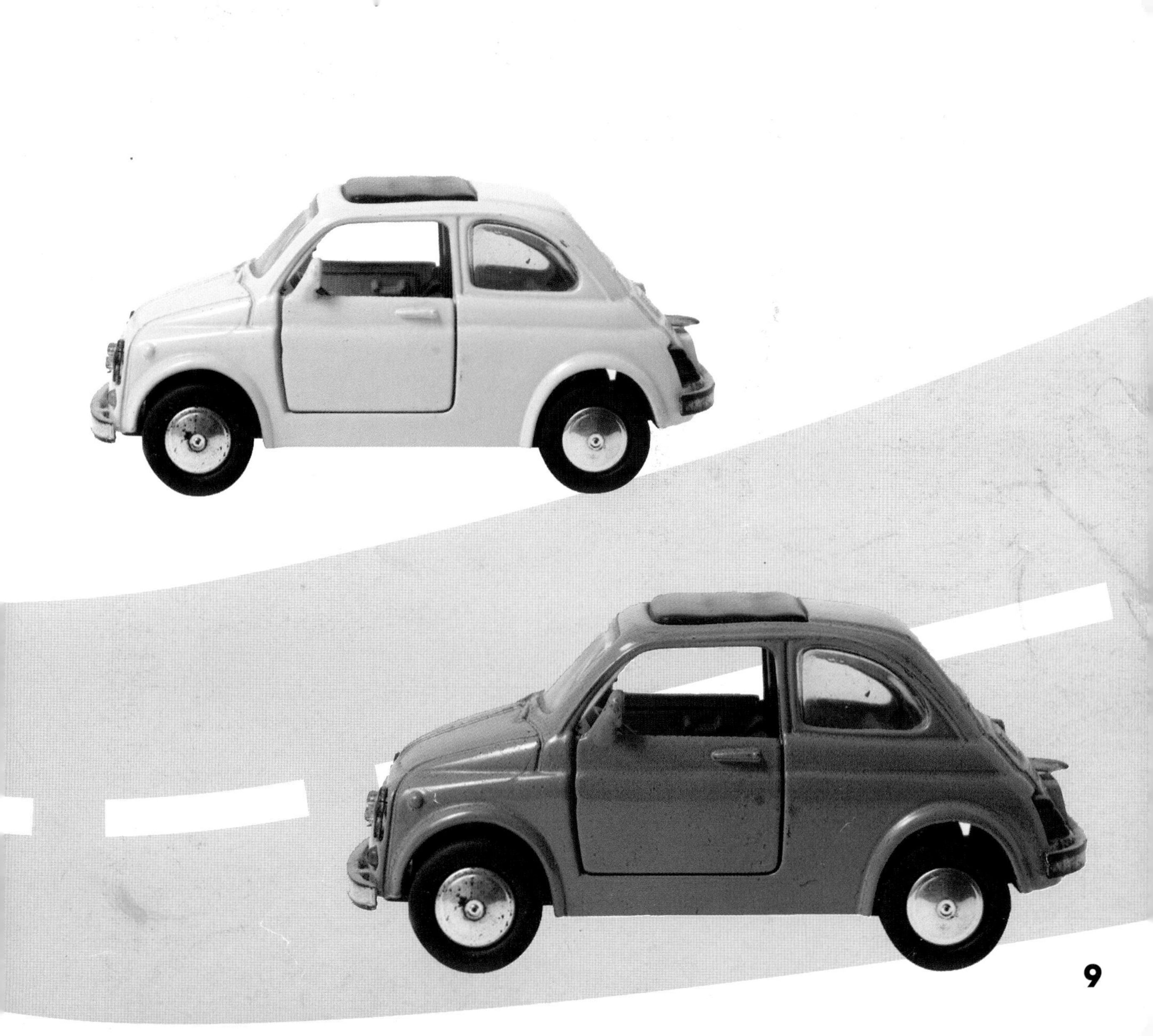

I have 3 blocks.

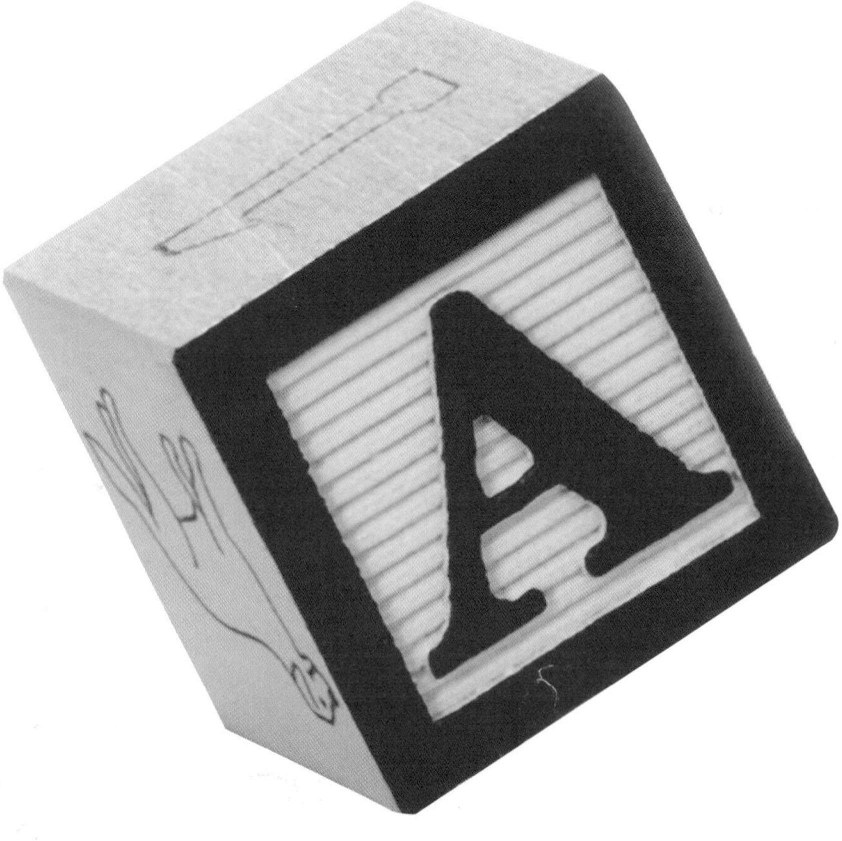

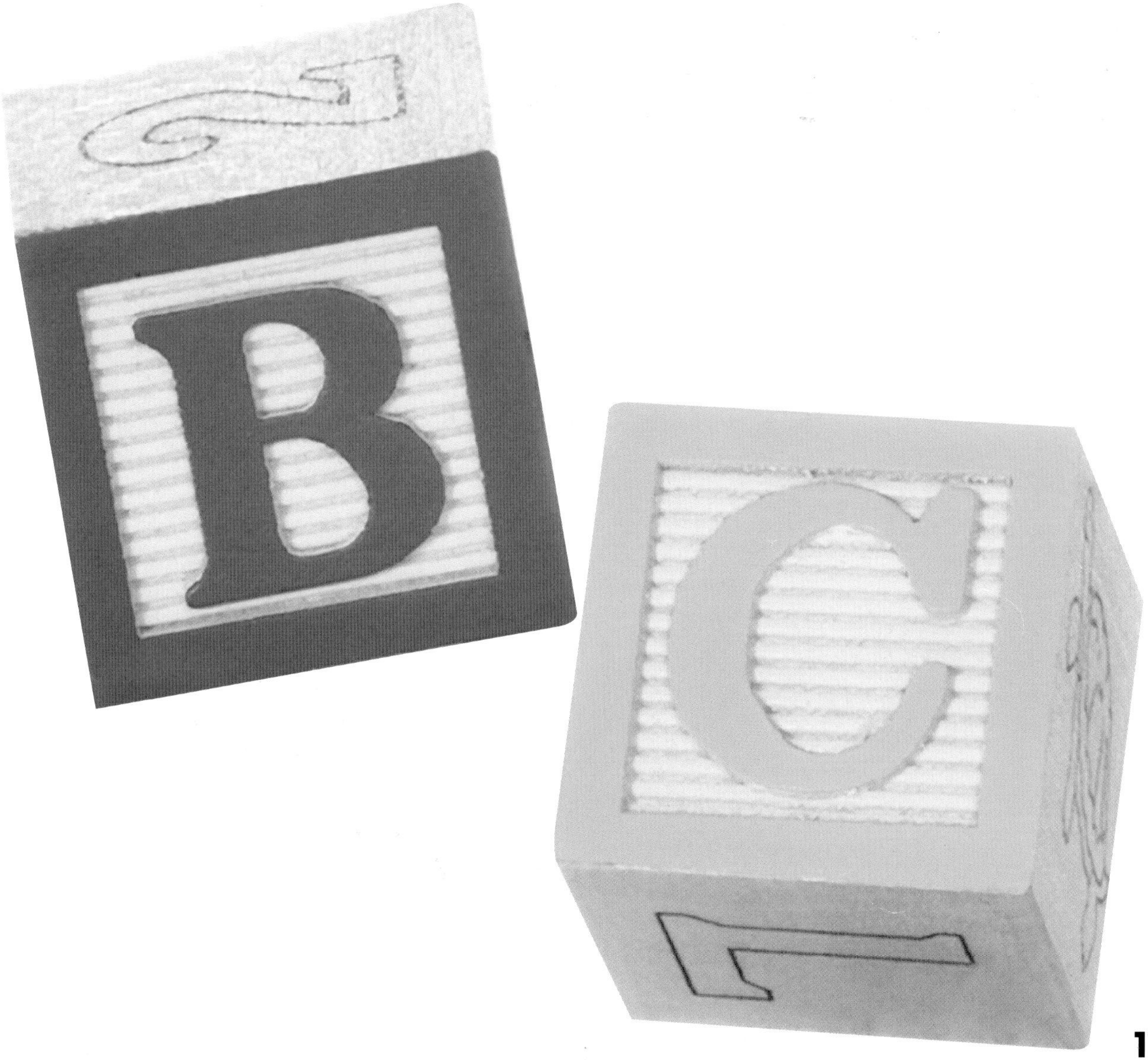

I have 2 puzzles.

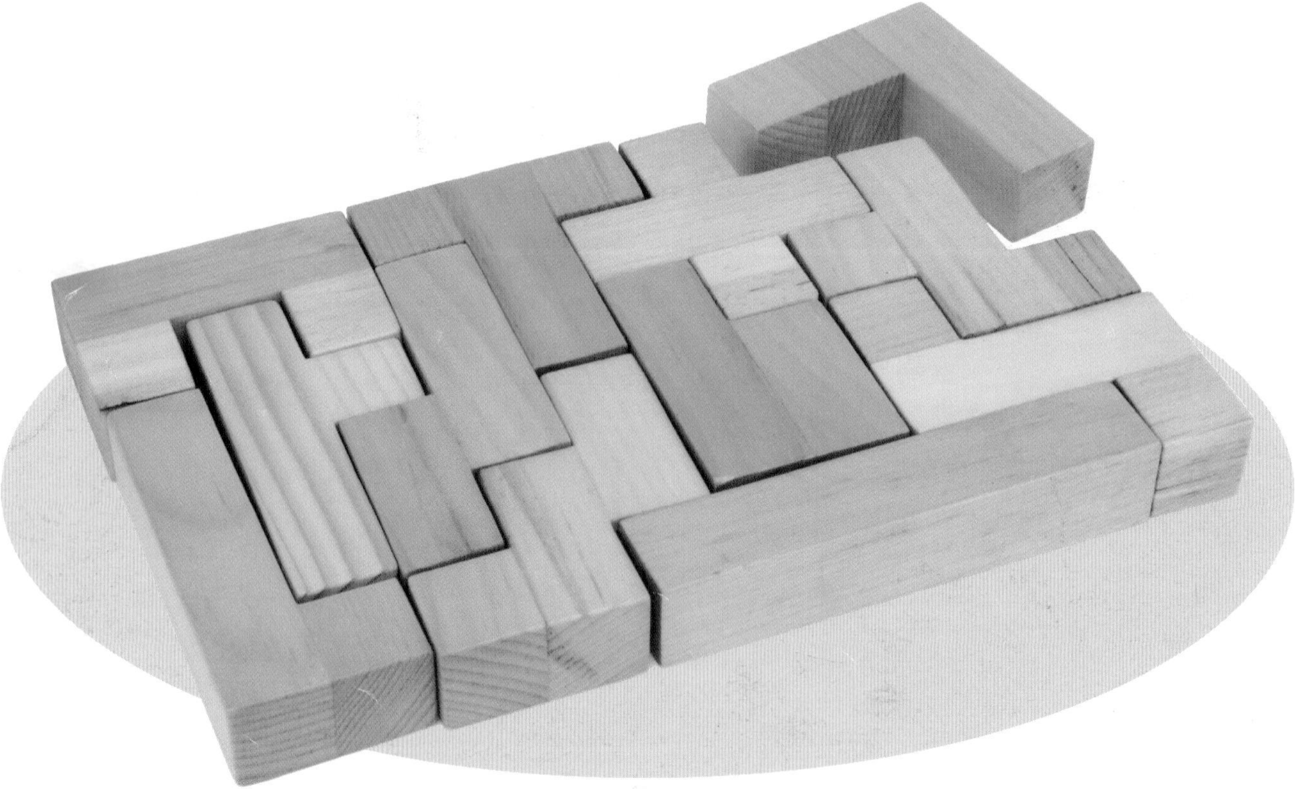

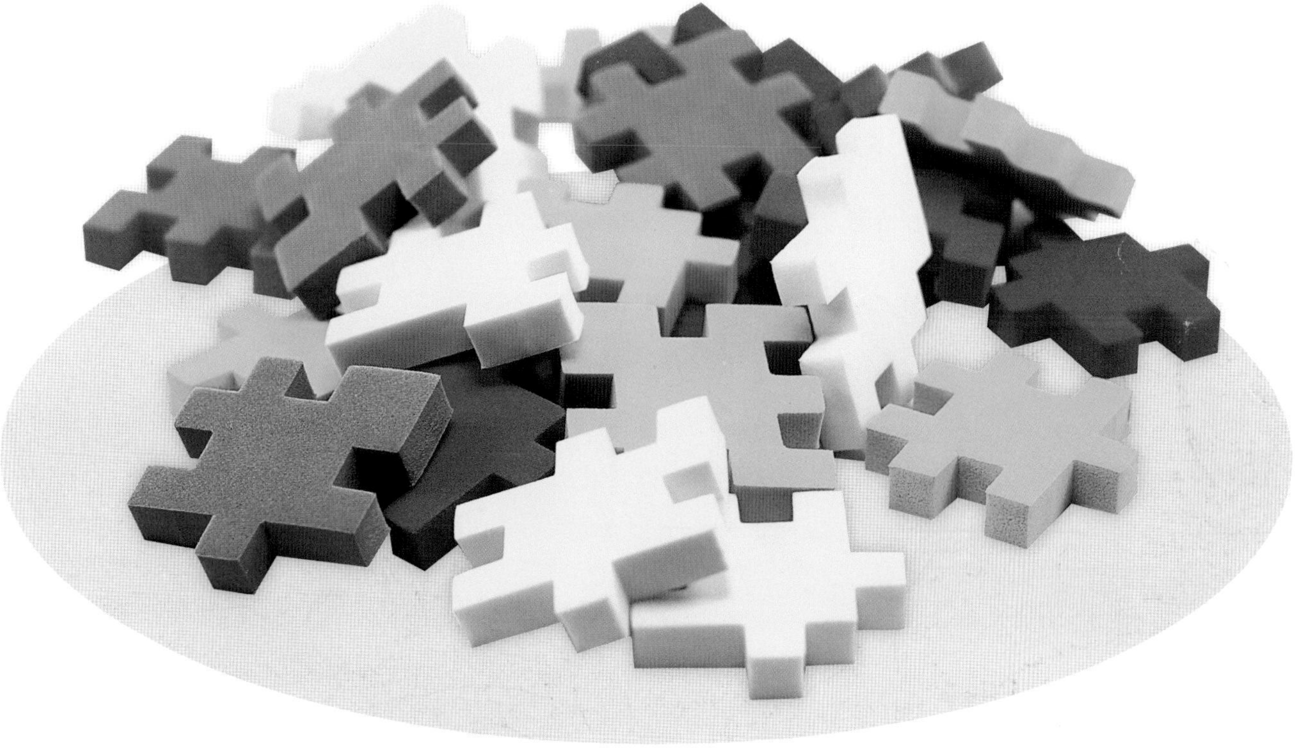

I have 1 jump rope.

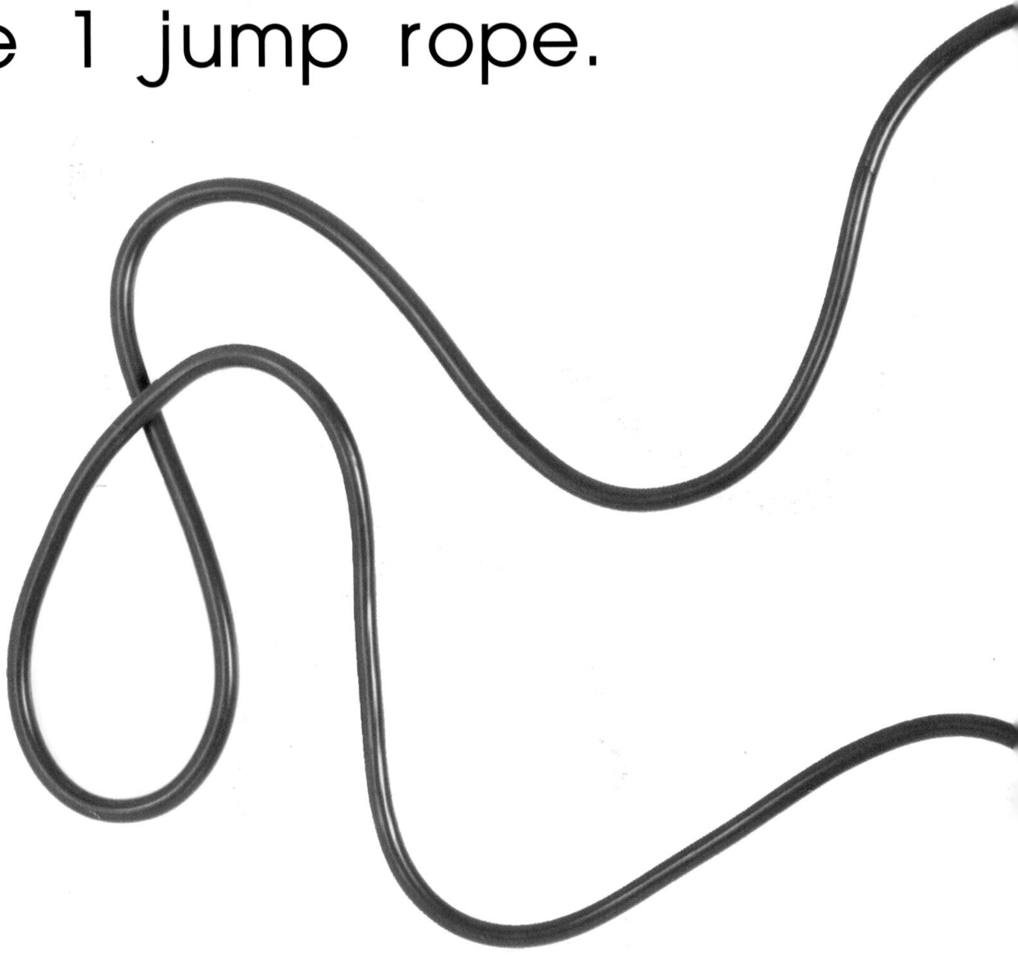

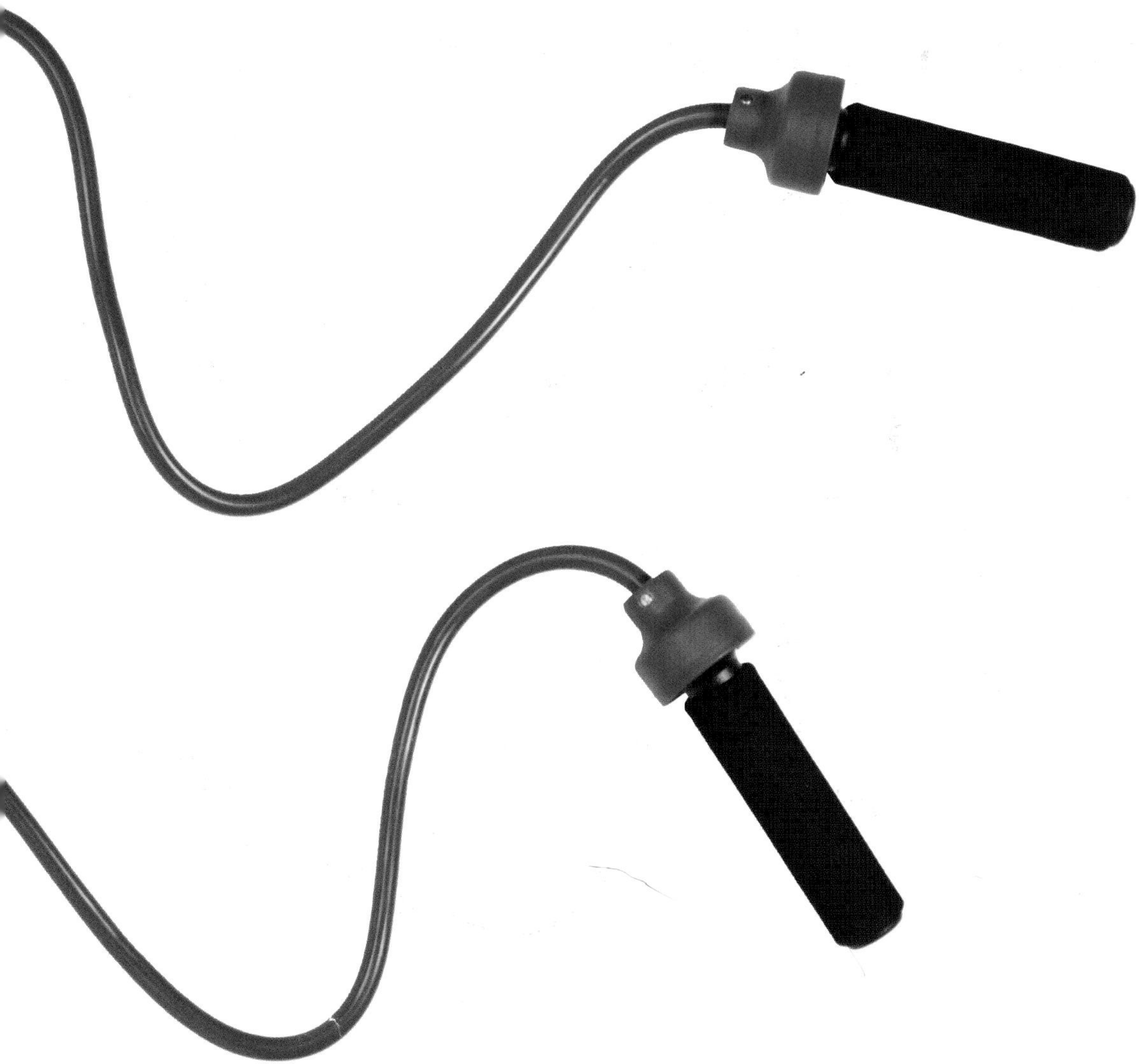

I have 1 toy box.

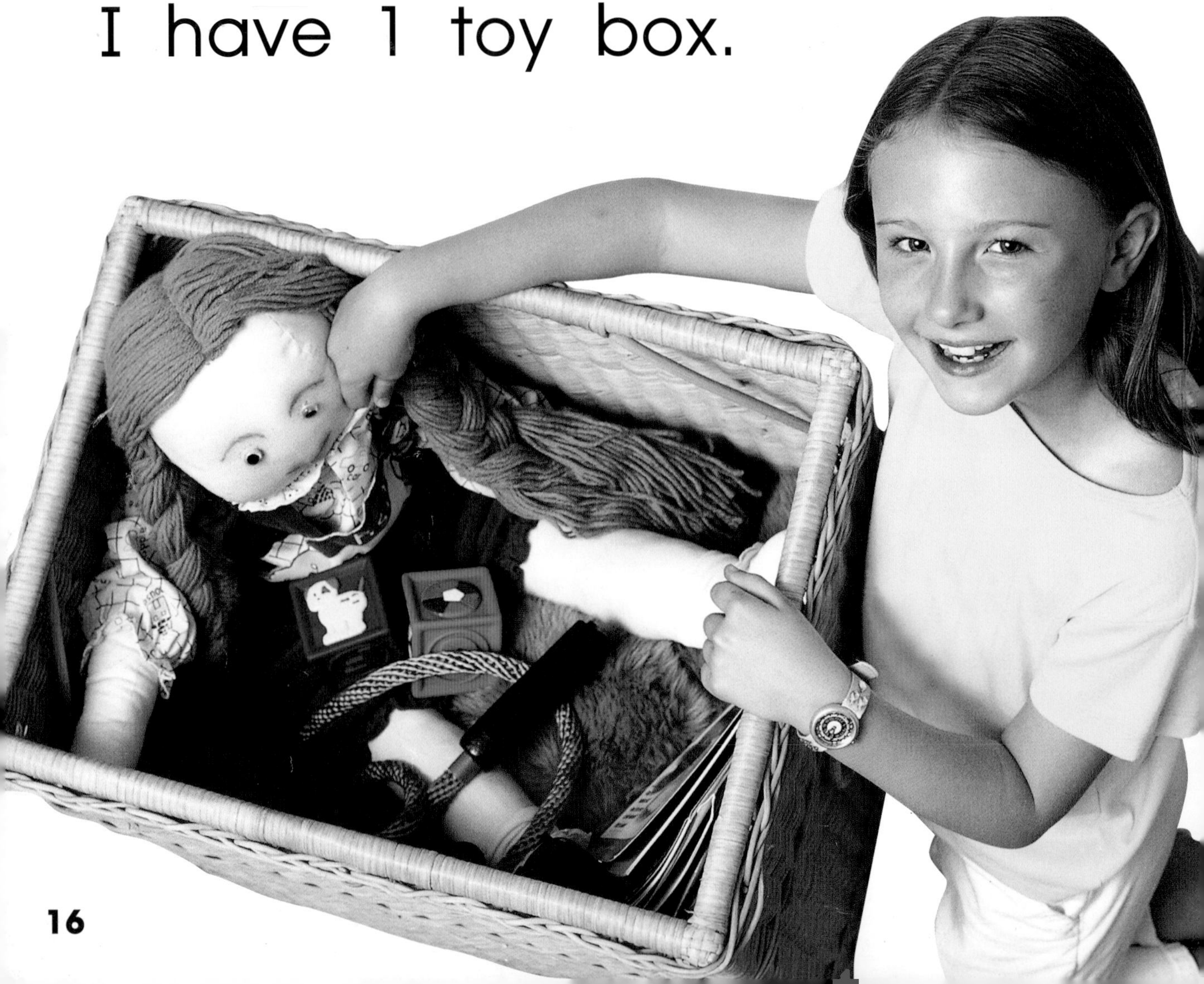